Copyright 2024 by Maxwell Sterling

Published by Yaskey Productions. LLC

All rights reserved.

Welcome to "TikTok Sales Mastery: Unlocking Viral Success." In the fast-paced world of social media, TikTok has emerged as a powerhouse platform that offers unparalleled opportunities for building an audience, driving engagement, and creating income streams. Whether you're a small business owner, an aspiring entrepreneur, or simply looking to increase your online presence, understanding how to leverage TikTok is essential for success in today's digital landscape.

The Power of TikTok

TikTok's meteoric rise is nothing short of phenomenal. Since its launch in 2016, the platform has amassed over 1 billion monthly active users globally, with a significant portion of its user base aged between 20-42. This demographic is particularly valuable as it represents a group with substantial purchasing power and a keen interest in discovering new products and trends (Jungle Scout) (Sprout Social) (Social Media Dashboard). According to Statista, 32% of TikTok's global active users are between the ages of 25 and 34, and 67% are 18-24, highlighting the platform's reach among young adults with disposable income (Sprout Social) (Social Champ).

But it's not just the user numbers that make TikTok a game-changer. The platform's unique algorithm is designed to promote content organically, enabling even new users to go viral overnight. Unlike other social media platforms that prioritize content from established accounts, TikTok offers a level playing field where creativity and engagement are the ultimate currencies. This means that with the right strategy, you can reach millions of potential customers without a massive advertising budget (Social Media Dashboard) (Social Champ).

The TikTok Algorithm vs. Other Social Media Algorithms

But it's not just the user numbers that make TikTok a game-changer. The platform's unique algorithm is designed to promote content organically, enabling even new users to go viral overnight. This democratized approach sets TikTok apart from other social media platforms and can significantly benefit businesses and creators who are just starting out.

How TikTok's Algorithm Works

TikTok's algorithm evaluates videos based on several factors, including user interactions (likes, comments, shares, and follows), video information (captions, sounds, and hashtags), and device and account settings (language preference, device type, and location) (Social Media Dashboard). Importantly, it prioritizes content relevance and engagement over the follower count of the account posting the video. This means that even if you have a small following, your content can still be pushed to a large audience if it resonates with viewers.

Comparison with Other Platforms

In contrast, platforms like Facebook and Instagram tend to prioritize content from accounts with larger followings or higher engagement histories. This often makes it difficult for new users to gain traction without substantial investment in advertising. For example, Instagram's algorithm heavily favors posts from accounts that users already interact with frequently, which can limit the visibility of new content creators (Social Media Dashboard) (Social Champ).

Level Playing Field for Creativity and Engagement

TikTok offers a level playing field where creativity and engagement are the ultimate currencies. This opens up opportunities for small businesses and new creators to reach millions of potential customers without a massive advertising budget. The virality of TikTok content is not just a theory; it is a well-documented phenomenon. For instance, Nathan Apodaca, a TikTok user who went viral for his cranberry juice skateboarding video, gained millions of followers overnight and received brand deals from multiple companies (Sprout Social) (Social Media Dashboard).

Proven Success Stories

Recent studies highlight the significant impact TikTok can have on sales and brand awareness. For instance, a survey by Adweek found that 49% of TikTok users have purchased a product after seeing it advertised, promoted, or reviewed on the platform (Social Media Dashboard). Moreover, brands that actively engage on TikTok see a 15% increase in their follower base each month, demonstrating the platform's effectiveness in building a loyal audience (Social Champ). Another study from Kantar showed that TikTok ads are more likely to lead to action compared to ads on other platforms, with a 1.5x higher purchase intent (Kalodata).

By leveraging TikTok's algorithm, businesses and creators can maximize their reach and engagement, turning viral moments into tangible business outcomes. This book will guide you through the strategies and best practices needed to succeed on this dynamic platform.

Addressing Common Frustrations

For many content creators, entrepreneurs, social media influencers, and affiliate marketers, the journey to online success is often fraught with frustration. Competing algorithms, expensive courses, and a constantly changing social media landscape can make it difficult to gain traction and see real results. Many have invested time and money into mastering platforms like Facebook and Instagram, only to find their content buried under that of more established accounts or overshadowed by paid promotions.

TikTok, however, offers a unique opportunity to bypass these barriers. The platform's algorithm doesn't just favor the already popular; it actively seeks out and promotes fresh, engaging content. This democratized approach means that with creativity and strategic posting, anyone can achieve viral success.

Why This Book?

In "TikTok Sales Mastery," you'll discover actionable strategies and insights that will help you harness the full potential of TikTok without needing to sign up for expensive courses. This book serves as your comprehensive guide, offering practical steps and expert advice to help you navigate the platform effectively. From setting up your account and creating compelling content to leveraging influencer partnerships and running effective ad campaigns, this book covers every aspect of TikTok marketing. Our goal is to provide you with a roadmap that not only educates but also inspires you to take action and achieve your business goals.

By following the strategies outlined in this book, you can build a substantial following, increase engagement, and drive sales, all without breaking the bank. Whether you're just starting out or looking to refine your existing strategy, "TikTok Sales Mastery" is the essential resource you need to succeed in the dynamic world of TikTok.

Chapter 1: Setting Up for Success

To succeed on TikTok, you need a solid foundation. This chapter will guide you through the essential steps to set up your TikTok account for business success, ensuring you start on the right foot.

Creating a Pro Account

The first step in your TikTok journey is to create a Pro account. TikTok offers two types of Pro accounts: Creator and Business. Both types provide access to detailed analytics and other tools that are crucial for growing your presence on the platform.

- **Steps to Switch to a Pro Account**:
    1. Download the TikTok app and create a new account or log in to your existing one.

2. Go to your profile and tap the three dots in the top right corner to access settings.
3. Select "Manage Account" and then "Switch to Pro Account."
4. Choose between a Creator or Business account based on your needs. If you're focused on brand growth and sales, a Business account is typically the best choice.

Switching to a Pro account is free and unlocks valuable features like audience insights, performance metrics, and advertising options (Jungle Scout) (Sprout Social).

Building a Professional Profile

Your profile is the first impression potential followers and customers will have of your brand on TikTok. It's essential to make it count. A well-crafted profile can significantly enhance your visibility, credibility, and engagement. Here are detailed steps to ensure your profile stands out:

Choosing a Consistent Username

Your username is a key element of your TikTok identity. It should be:

- **Consistent with Your Branding**: Use the same username across all your social media platforms to ensure brand consistency and make it easier for users to find and recognize you. For example, if your brand is called "HealthyBites," your username should be @HealthyBites on TikTok, Instagram, Twitter, etc.

8

- **Easy to Remember and Spell**: Avoid complicated spellings or special characters that can confuse your audience. A straightforward, memorable username increases the likelihood that users will search for and follow you.
- **Reflective of Your Brand**: Your username should give an indication of what your brand is about. If you're a fitness brand, a name like @FitLifeTips would be more appropriate than something vague like @John123.

Pro Tip: Use a tool like Namechk or Knowem to check the availability of your desired username across multiple platforms simultaneously.

Crafting a Compelling Bio

Your bio is a concise summary of who you are and what you offer. It should include:

- **A Clear Description of Your Brand**: Briefly explain what you do and what makes you unique. For instance, "Bringing you daily fitness tips and healthy recipes" clearly conveys the purpose of a fitness brand.
- **Keywords**: Incorporate relevant keywords that your target audience might use to find content like yours. This can improve your discoverability within the app.
- **A Call-to-Action (CTA)**: Encourage visitors to take action, such as visiting your website, signing up for a newsletter, or checking out

your latest product. Example: "Check out our latest fitness gear! Link below."
- **Contact Information**: Provide a way for potential customers or collaborators to reach you, such as an email address or a link to your contact page.

What to Include:

- Clear and concise description of your brand.
- Keywords relevant to your niche.
- A strong CTA.
- Contact information or links.

What to Avoid:

- Overly long descriptions.
- Irrelevant information.
- Excessive use of emojis or special characters that can make your bio look cluttered.

Pro Tip: Regularly update your bio to reflect current promotions, new products, or significant changes in your brand focus.

Connecting Other Social Media Accounts

Linking your other social media accounts to your TikTok profile is essential for cross-promotion and growing your overall online presence. Here's how to do it:

- **Instagram and YouTube Integration:**
    1. Go to your TikTok profile and tap "Edit profile."
    2. Select "Add Instagram" and "Add YouTube."
    3. Log in to your accounts and authorize TikTok to connect.
- **Why Link Other Accounts:**
    - **Increased Visibility:** Followers on TikTok can easily discover your other content, helping to grow your audience on multiple platforms.
    - **Consistent Branding:** Maintain a unified brand presence across all social media.
    - **Engagement Opportunities:** Drive traffic to your longer-form content on YouTube or your photo-centric content on Instagram.

Pro Tip: Regularly remind your TikTok followers to check out your other social media accounts by mentioning them in your videos and including direct links in your bio.

By following these steps and best practices, you'll be well on your way to establishing a strong, professional presence on TikTok. This foundation will not only make your profile more attractive to potential followers but also increase your chances of turning viewers into loyal customers. In the next chapter, you'll dive into creating high-quality content that resonates with your audience and leverages current trends to boost your visibility and engagement.

Best Practices for Setting Up Your Profile

Setting up a professional and engaging profile is a crucial step in building your TikTok presence. Here are detailed steps to make these best practices easier and more effective:

Profile Picture

Your profile picture is one of the first things users will notice about your account. It should be:

- **High-Quality**: Use a clear, high-resolution image. Blurry or pixelated images can make your profile look unprofessional.
- **Brand-Representative**: Choose an image that accurately represents your brand. This could be your company logo if you're a business, or a professional photo if you're an individual creator. For personal brands, a well-lit, friendly headshot works best.
- **Consistent Across Platforms**: Use the same profile picture on all your social media accounts to maintain brand consistency and make it easier for users to recognize you across different platforms.

Pro Tip: If you're using a logo, ensure it is centered and clearly visible in the small circular frame that TikTok uses for profile pictures. Avoid using too much text or intricate details that may not be legible.

Bio Links

TikTok allows you to add links to your bio, which is a valuable feature for driving traffic to your website, online store, or other social media profiles.

- **How to Add Links**:
    1. Go to your profile and tap "Edit profile."
    2. In the "Website" field, enter the URL you want to link to.
- **What to Link**:
    - **TikTok Shop**: If you have a TikTok Shop, include the link to make it easy for users to browse and purchase your products directly from your profile.
    - **Website or Blog**: Drive traffic to your main website or blog where users can learn more about your brand or services.
    - **Other Social Media Accounts**: Cross-promote by linking your Instagram, YouTube, or Twitter accounts. This can help grow your overall following.

Pro Tip: Use link shorteners like Bitly or Linktree to create clean, trackable links. Linktree allows you to create a single URL that directs users to a landing page with multiple links, which is useful if you have several pages you want to promote.

Contact Information

Providing contact information in your profile is essential for potential customers or collaborators to reach you easily.

- **What to Include:**
    - **Business Email**: A professional email address where users can contact you for business inquiries, collaborations, or customer support.
    - **Phone Number**: If applicable, a business phone number can also be included, though email is often preferred for initial contact.
    - **Additional Contact Methods**: You can also include links to contact forms or messaging apps like WhatsApp or Telegram if they are part of your communication strategy.
- **How to Add Contact Information**:
    - Go to your profile and tap "Edit profile."
    - In the "Bio" section, add your contact details. You can use a format like "For business inquiries: [email@example.com]".

Pro Tip: Keep your contact information up-to-date. Regularly check the provided email and phone number to ensure they are working and monitored.

Case Study #1: Optimized Profile Setup

Consider the case of "Nature's Glow Skincare," a small skincare brand that effectively set up their TikTok profile to enhance their online presence and attract a dedicated following. By focusing on a professional and inviting profile, Nature's Glow Skincare was able to drive engagement, increase their customer base, and grow their business significantly. Here's how they did it:

Profile Picture

Nature's Glow Skincare used a high-resolution image of their logo as their profile picture. This choice was crucial for several reasons:

- **Brand Consistency**: The same logo is used across all their social media accounts, which helps in maintaining a cohesive brand image and making it easier for users to recognize them across different platforms.
- **Professional Appeal**: A clear and professional logo conveys credibility and trustworthiness, essential qualities for a skincare brand aiming to attract customers who value quality and reliability.

Pro Tip: Ensure that your logo or profile picture is centered and easily recognizable in the small circular frame used by TikTok. Avoid overly intricate designs that may not be visible on small screens.

Bio Links

Nature's Glow Skincare effectively utilized the bio link feature to drive traffic to multiple important online destinations:

- **Linktree Integration**: Their bio includes a Linktree URL, which provides a centralized hub for multiple links. This setup directs users to:

- **TikTok Shop**: Allowing followers to browse and purchase products directly within the app.
- **Main Website**: Offering more detailed information about their products, company history, and additional content such as blogs and skincare tips.
- **Instagram Profile**: Encouraging cross-platform engagement and showcasing a more extensive portfolio of their products through photos and videos.

Pro Tip: Use link management tools like Linktree to create a single URL that hosts multiple links. This approach helps you efficiently direct traffic to various channels and makes it easy for users to find what they're looking for.

Contact Information

Nature's Glow Skincare included a professional email address in their TikTok bio, making it easy for potential customers and business partners to reach out:

- **Business Email**: A dedicated email address for business inquiries (e.g., contact@naturesglow.com) helps in organizing communication and ensuring that important messages are not missed.
- **Additional Contact Methods**: They also provided links to a contact form on their website, catering to users who might prefer reaching out through a form rather than direct email.

Pro Tip: Regularly monitor the provided email address and ensure that inquiries are responded to promptly. This demonstrates professionalism and commitment to customer service.

Content Strategy and Engagement

Beyond setting up a professional profile, Nature's Glow Skincare adopted a strategic content approach that maximized their engagement and growth on TikTok:

- **Educational Content**: They posted videos offering skincare tips, ingredient spotlights, and product usage tutorials. This not only highlighted the benefits of their products but also positioned them as an authority in the skincare industry.
- **User-Generated Content**: Encouraging customers to share their experiences and results using Nature's Glow products helped create authentic testimonials and build community trust.
- **Trending Challenges and Hashtags**: They participated in popular TikTok challenges and used trending hashtags relevant to skincare and beauty, increasing their visibility and attracting new followers.

Pro Tip: Engage with your audience by responding to comments, participating in trends, and encouraging user-generated content. This interaction not only boosts your visibility but also fosters a loyal community around your brand.

Results and Impact

By following these best practices, Nature's Glow Skincare built a professional and inviting TikTok profile that attracted followers and facilitated business growth. The results of their optimized profile and strategic content included:

- **Increased Follower Count**: Their follower count grew steadily as more users discovered their informative and engaging content.
- **Boost in Online Sales**: The direct link to their TikTok Shop and main website in their bio facilitated easy access for users to purchase products, leading to a significant increase in online sales.
- **Enhanced Brand Loyalty**: Regular engagement with their audience helped build a loyal customer base that not only followed their content but also actively promoted their products through word-of-mouth and user-generated content.

By focusing on these key areas—profile picture, bio links, and contact information—Nature's Glow Skincare successfully created a compelling and professional TikTok profile. This foundational setup was crucial for building a successful presence on TikTok and converting followers into loyal customers. Following their example can help you achieve similar success and leverage TikTok's powerful platform to grow your brand.

Case Study #2: Successful Profile Setup

Consider the case of GymShark, a fitness apparel brand that has effectively leveraged TikTok to increase its visibility and sales. By creating a compelling profile, posting engaging content, and actively participating in TikTok trends, GymShark grew its following to over 2 million users and significantly boosted its online sales.

Profile Picture

GymShark uses a high-resolution image of its logo as the profile picture. This simple yet effective strategy ensures brand consistency across all platforms. The logo is clean, easily recognizable, and aligned with GymShark's branding, making it instantly identifiable to their audience.

Compelling Bio

GymShark's TikTok bio is concise and impactful. It includes a brief description of the brand, "Official GymShark - Conditioning Apparel Innovators," which immediately tells users what the brand is about. They also include a call-to-action with a link to their online store, making it easy for followers to explore and purchase their products.

- **Keywords and Call-to-Action**: The bio incorporates keywords related to fitness and apparel, which helps in searchability and relevance. The call-to-action, "Shop the latest collections," directs traffic to their website, facilitating conversions.

Bio Links

GymShark takes advantage of the link feature in their bio by including a Linktree URL. This link directs users to multiple destinations, including their main website, online store, Instagram profile, and YouTube channel. This multi-link approach maximizes cross-platform engagement and sales opportunities.

- **Linktree Integration**: Using Linktree allows GymShark to promote various aspects of their brand and provides followers with easy access to their content and products, enhancing the user experience and driving traffic across their online presence.

Contact Information

GymShark includes contact information in their bio, making it easy for potential customers and collaborators to reach out. They provide a professional email address for business inquiries, ensuring that they are accessible for partnerships, customer service, and other business opportunities.

Content Strategy

GymShark's content strategy on TikTok is a blend of educational, motivational, and entertaining videos. They frequently post workout routines, fitness tips, and motivational content that resonates with their target audience. This strategy not only promotes their products but also positions GymShark as an authority in the fitness industry.

- **Trending Hashtags and Challenges**: GymShark actively participates in trending hashtags and challenges, which increases their content's visibility. By leveraging popular trends, they tap into broader audiences and enhance their chances of going viral.
- **User-Generated Content**: They encourage their followers to share videos wearing GymShark apparel with specific hashtags, creating a community-driven content stream. This not only increases engagement but also serves as authentic testimonials for their products.

Analytics and Optimization

GymShark regularly monitors their TikTok analytics to understand what type of content performs best. They track metrics such as video views, engagement rates, and follower growth to refine their strategy continuously. This data-driven approach allows them to optimize their content for maximum impact.

- **Performance Metrics**: By analyzing which videos receive the most engagement, GymShark can replicate successful content themes and formats, ensuring a consistent stream of high-performing videos.

Results and Impact

Through these strategic efforts, GymShark has successfully grown its TikTok following to over 2 million users. This substantial audience base has translated into increased brand awareness and significant boosts in online sales. Their active engagement with the TikTok community has also helped in building a loyal customer base that actively promotes their brand.

- **Increased Sales**: The direct link to their online store in the bio, coupled with engaging content, has driven significant traffic and conversions, contributing to the overall growth of their e-commerce sales.
- **Brand Loyalty**: By fostering a community of fitness enthusiasts, GymShark has built a strong, loyal following that continuously engages with their content and promotes their products.

By following GymShark's example and implementing these best practices, you can effectively establish a strong presence on TikTok, engage with your target audience, and drive substantial business growth. The foundation you set with a compelling profile and strategic content will pave the way for your success on the platform.

By following these steps and best practices, you'll be well on your way to establishing a strong presence on TikTok and setting the stage for your business success.

Chapter 2: Content Creation and Trends

Creating high-quality content and staying up-to-date with current trends are essential for success on TikTok. In this chapter, we'll dive into the key elements of producing engaging videos and leveraging trending topics to boost your visibility and engagement.

Producing High-Quality Content

Producing high-quality content on TikTok involves several crucial elements that can significantly enhance your videos' performance and appeal. Let's explore these elements in detail:

Elements of a Successful TikTok Video

1. **Engaging Visuals**:
    - **High-Resolution Video**: Ensure your videos are clear and visually appealing. Use good lighting and avoid shaky footage to maintain a professional look.
    - **Interesting Backgrounds**: Incorporate visually stimulating backgrounds or settings relevant to your content. A clean, well-organized environment can make your videos more attractive.
2. **Quick Hooks**:
    - **Grab Attention Immediately**: The first few seconds of your video are crucial. Start with an eye-catching moment or intriguing statement to capture viewers' attention. For example, begin with a surprising fact or a visually striking action.
    - **Clear Purpose**: Make sure the purpose of the video is apparent from the start. Whether it's a tutorial, a product showcase, or a fun challenge, clarity helps retain viewers.
3. **Trending Sounds**:
    - **Popular Audio Clips**: Use trending sounds and music to make your videos more discoverable. TikTok's algorithm often promotes content that uses popular audio clips, increasing your chances of reaching a broader audience (Social Media Dashboard) (Kalodata).

- **Sound Quality**: Ensure the audio is clear and balanced. Background noise can be distracting and reduce the quality of your video.

Examples of Viral Content:

- **Dance Challenges**: Simple, catchy dance routines set to popular music often go viral. Users enjoy recreating these dances, which helps your video spread.
- **Tutorials and How-To Videos**: Quick, informative videos that teach a skill or provide valuable information tend to attract a lot of attention. Ensure the instructions are clear and concise.
- **Before and After Transformations**: These videos, especially in beauty, fitness, or home improvement niches, captivate viewers by showing dramatic changes.

Leveraging Current Trends

Staying current with trends is a powerful way to increase your visibility on TikTok. Here's how to effectively identify and participate in trends:

Identifying and Participating in Trending Challenges and Hashtags

1. **Monitoring Trends**:
    - **Discover Page**: Regularly check TikTok's Discover page to see the latest trending hashtags and challenges. This page highlights what's popular on the platform, giving you

insight into what content is gaining traction (Sprout Social) (Social Media Dashboard).
- **Follow Influencers**: Keep an eye on popular influencers in your niche. They often set or participate in trends early, providing you with ideas for your content.

2. **Participating in Challenges**:
   - **Relevance**: Choose challenges that are relevant to your brand or personal interests. Authenticity is key; forced participation in unrelated trends can seem disingenuous.
   - **Creativity**: Put your unique spin on trends. While participating in challenges, add your personal touch or brand elements to stand out from the crowd.

3. **Using Trending Hashtags**:
   - **Appropriate Hashtags**: Use trending hashtags that align with your content. Overloading your video with irrelevant hashtags can be seen as spammy and might not help your visibility.
   - **Combine Popular and Niche Hashtags**: Mix widely used hashtags with more specific ones to reach both broad and targeted audiences.

Using TikTok's Discover Page and Trending Audio Clips

1. **Exploring the Discover Page**:
   - **Trending Topics**: The Discover page showcases trending topics and popular hashtags. Engage with these topics by creating relevant content.

- **Audience Preferences**: The page can give you insights into what your audience might be interested in, helping you tailor your content accordingly.
2. **Incorporating Trending Audio Clips**:
    - **Viral Sounds**: Using audio clips that are currently viral can increase your content's reach. TikTok's algorithm favors videos that use popular sounds, pushing them to a wider audience (Kalodata).
    - **Creative Use**: Be creative in how you incorporate trending sounds. Whether through lip-syncing, acting out scenes, or using them as background music for your tutorials, make sure it adds value to your video.

Pro Tip: Keep an eye on TikTok's notifications for trend alerts and explore the "For You" page regularly to see what types of content are currently performing well.

By producing high-quality content and leveraging current trends effectively, you can significantly enhance your TikTok presence. Remember, the key is to be authentic, creative, and consistent. In the next chapter, we will delve deeper into engagement strategies that will help you build a loyal following and drive your TikTok success even further.

Chapter 3: Engagement Strategies

Engagement is the lifeblood of TikTok success. Capturing and maintaining your audience's attention requires strategic planning and execution. This chapter covers techniques for making an immediate impact and maintaining a consistent posting schedule.

Capturing Attention Quickly

In the fast-paced world of TikTok, grabbing your audience's attention in the first few seconds is crucial. Here are some techniques to ensure your videos hook viewers right from the start:

Techniques for Making an Impact in the First Few Seconds

1. **Start with a Bang**:
   - **Surprising Elements**: Begin your video with something unexpected or intriguing to pique curiosity. This could be a surprising fact, a dramatic action, or an eye-catching visual.
   - **Bold Statements**: Use powerful and provocative statements to immediately draw viewers in. For example, "Did you know this simple trick can double your productivity?" can be an effective hook.

2. **Dynamic Visuals**:
   - **Fast-Paced Editing**: Quick cuts and dynamic transitions can keep viewers engaged. Avoid slow intros or prolonged scenes that might lose their interest.
   - **High-Quality Imagery**: Ensure your visuals are clear and vibrant. Poor video quality can turn viewers away before they even get to the core of your content.

3. **Engaging Thumbnails**:
   - **Eye-Catching Thumbnails**: The cover image for your video should be compelling and relevant. Use bright colors, clear images, and text overlays to attract clicks.

Case Studies of Successful Videos with Strong Initial Hooks:

- **Case Study 1: Sarah's Fitness Tips**: Sarah, a fitness influencer, starts her videos with high-energy moves and immediate value. Her video "Quick Tips for a Flat Stomach" begins with a dynamic

workout routine, grabbing viewers' attention and encouraging them to watch till the end.
- **Case Study 2: Tech Guru's Gadget Reviews**: A tech reviewer known as Tech Guru opens his videos with a bold statement or question like, "Is this the best smartphone of 2024?" followed by a quick, flashy montage of the gadget's highlights. This approach has significantly boosted his viewership and engagement rates ([Sprout Social](#)) ([Social Media Dashboard](#)).

Consistent Posting

Consistency is key to maintaining visibility and engagement on TikTok. Here's why regular posting matters and how to develop an effective content calendar.

Importance of Regular Posting

- **Algorithm Favorability**: TikTok's algorithm favors accounts that post frequently. Consistent posting increases your chances of being featured on the "For You" page, which can significantly boost your visibility.
- **Audience Expectation**: Regular posts help in building and retaining a loyal audience. When followers expect and receive regular content, they are more likely to stay engaged with your profile.

Developing a Content Calendar and Scheduling Posts for Optimal Times

1. **Create a Content Calendar:**
   - **Planning Ahead**: Outline your content ideas for the week or month ahead. This helps in maintaining a steady flow of posts without scrambling for last-minute ideas.
   - **Variety and Balance**: Mix different types of content such as tutorials, behind-the-scenes, user-generated content, and trend participation to keep your feed diverse and engaging.
2. **Scheduling Posts:**
   - **Optimal Posting Times**: Research indicates that the best times to post on TikTok are generally in the evening when users are more active. However, analyze your own analytics to find the optimal times specific to your audience.
   - **Use Scheduling Tools**: Utilize tools like Hootsuite or Later to schedule your posts. This ensures consistency even when you're busy with other tasks.

Pro Tip: TikTok recommends posting 1-4 times per day, but quality should not be compromised for quantity. Start with 3-5 posts per week and gradually increase frequency as you get comfortable ([Social Media Dashboard](#)) ([Social Champ](#)).

Chapter 4: Influencer Collaborations

Collaborating with influencers can significantly amplify your reach and credibility on TikTok. This chapter will guide you through identifying the right influencers and maximizing these partnerships for business growth.

Finding the Right Influencers

Identifying influencers who align with your brand and target audience is crucial for effective collaborations. Here's how to find the perfect match:

How to Identify Influencers that Align with Your Brand Ethos and Target Audience

1. **Research and Discovery:**
    - **Niche Relevance**: Look for influencers within your industry or niche. Use TikTok's search function, explore

hashtags, and browse the Discover page to find potential collaborators.
- **Audience Demographics**: Ensure the influencer's audience demographics match your target market. Tools like Social Blade or HypeAuditor can provide insights into an influencer's follower base and engagement rates.

2. **Evaluate Content and Engagement:**
   - **Content Quality**: Analyze the quality of the influencer's content. High-quality, engaging content that aligns with your brand's values is essential.
   - **Engagement Rate**: Check the influencer's engagement rate (likes, comments, shares) rather than just follower count. High engagement indicates a loyal and active audience.

Strategies for Reaching Out and Collaborating Effectively

1. **Crafting a Compelling Pitch**:
   - **Personalized Approach**: Tailor your message to each influencer. Mention specific content of theirs that you enjoyed and explain why you think they'd be a great fit for your brand.
   - **Clear Value Proposition**: Highlight the benefits of the collaboration for the influencer. This could include financial compensation, free products, or exposure to your audience.

2. **Building Relationships**:
   - **Engage with Their Content**: Before reaching out, engage with the influencer's content by liking, commenting, and sharing. This shows genuine interest and can make your pitch more effective.
   - **Collaborative Flexibility**: Be open to the influencer's ideas and suggestions. They know their audience best, so their input can be invaluable for a successful partnership (Social Champ) (Kalodata).

Maximizing Influencer Partnerships

Once you've identified and secured an influencer collaboration, it's essential to maximize its potential.

Different Types of Collaborations

1. **Product Gifting**:
   - **Free Products**: Send free products to influencers for them to review or feature in their content. This is a cost-effective way to get authentic promotion.
   - **Unboxing Videos**: Encourage influencers to create unboxing videos, which can generate excitement and curiosity among their followers.
2. **Paid Partnerships**:
   - **Sponsored Content**: Pay influencers to create content that promotes your brand. Ensure the content feels authentic

and not overly commercialized to maintain trust with their audience.
- **Discount Codes**: Provide influencers with exclusive discount codes to share with their followers. This can drive sales and track the campaign's effectiveness.

3. **Co-Created Content**:
   - **Joint Campaigns**: Collaborate on content creation, such as challenges or series, where both the influencer and your brand are featured. This can create a more engaging and cohesive narrative.
   - **Live Streams**: Host live streams with influencers to interact with their audience in real-time. This can increase engagement and provide immediate feedback and interaction.

Measuring the Impact of Influencer Marketing on Sales and Engagement

1. **Track Performance Metrics**:
   - **Engagement Rates**: Monitor likes, comments, shares, and views on the influencer's posts about your brand. High engagement indicates successful collaboration.
   - **Sales and Traffic**: Use unique discount codes or trackable links to measure the direct impact on sales and website traffic from the influencer's promotion.

2. **Analyze Return on Investment (ROI)**:
    - **Cost vs. Benefit**: Compare the cost of the collaboration (products, payments) against the sales and new followers generated. A positive ROI indicates a successful campaign.
    - **Long-Term Impact**: Consider the long-term benefits such as increased brand awareness, follower growth, and customer loyalty that may not be immediately quantifiable (Social Champ) (Kalodata).

By following these strategies and best practices, you can effectively engage your audience and leverage influencer collaborations to drive growth on TikTok. In the next chapters, we will explore advanced advertising techniques and analytics to further enhance your TikTok marketing efforts.

Chapter 5: Advertising on TikTok

Advertising on TikTok is a powerful way to boost your brand's visibility, drive engagement, and increase sales. In this chapter, we will explore the various ad formats available on TikTok, best practices for creating effective ads, and strategies for budgeting and bidding to optimize your ad spend.

Overview of TikTok Ad Formats

TikTok offers several unique ad formats, each designed to engage users in different ways. Understanding these formats and how to use them effectively is crucial for running successful ad campaigns.

In-Feed Ads

In-feed ads appear in the user's "For You" feed as they scroll through content. These ads blend seamlessly with organic content, making them less intrusive and more engaging.

- **Characteristics**: Full-screen, sound-on, and support multiple call-to-actions (CTAs) such as app downloads, website visits, and purchases.
- **Best Practices**:
    - **Engaging Visuals**: Use high-quality images or videos that capture attention quickly.
    - **Clear CTAs**: Ensure your CTA is visible and compelling.
    - **Short and Sweet**: Keep your ad concise and to the point.

Brand Takeovers

Brand takeovers are full-screen ads that appear when a user opens the TikTok app. They can be static images, GIFs, or videos and usually include a clickable link to a landing page or a hashtag challenge.

- **Characteristics**: High visibility, exclusive to one advertiser per day.
- **Best Practices**:
    - **Eye-Catching Design**: Use bold visuals and clear messaging to make an immediate impact.
    - **Strong CTA**: Direct users to a specific action, such as visiting your website or participating in a challenge.

Hashtag Challenges

Hashtag challenges encourage users to create and share content based on a specific theme or task, using a branded hashtag.

- **Characteristics**: Highly engaging, user-generated content that can go viral.
- **Best Practices**:
    - **Clear Instructions**: Provide simple, easy-to-follow steps for users to participate.
    - **Incentives**: Offer rewards or incentives to encourage participation.
    - **Promotion**: Promote your challenge through other channels to increase awareness.

Budgeting and Bidding Strategies

Effective budgeting and bidding are essential for maximizing the return on your TikTok ad spend. Here's how to set a budget and optimize your bidding strategy:

Setting a Budget for TikTok Ads

- **Determine Your Goals**: Identify what you want to achieve with your ads (e.g., brand awareness, website traffic, sales) and allocate your budget accordingly.

- **Start Small**: Begin with a modest budget to test different ad formats and strategies. As you gather data on what works, you can increase your budget for more successful campaigns.
- **Daily vs. Total Budget**: Decide whether you want to set a daily budget (a fixed amount spent each day) or a total budget (the overall amount spent over the duration of the campaign). Both options have their advantages depending on your campaign goals.

Understanding the Bidding Process and Optimizing Ad Spend

- **Bidding Models**: TikTok offers several bidding models, including cost-per-click (CPC), cost-per-thousand-impressions (CPM), and optimized cost-per-click (oCPC). Choose the model that aligns best with your campaign goals.
- **Bid Adjustment**: Monitor your campaign performance and adjust your bids based on the results. Increase your bids for high-performing ads to maximize their reach.
- **A/B Testing**: Run A/B tests on different ad creatives, copy, and CTAs to determine what resonates most with your audience. Use the insights to optimize your future campaigns.

Pro Tip: Utilize TikTok's ad analytics tools to track your campaign performance and make data-driven decisions to enhance your ad effectiveness (Social Media Dashboard) (Social Champ).

Chapter 6: Setting Up a TikTok Shop

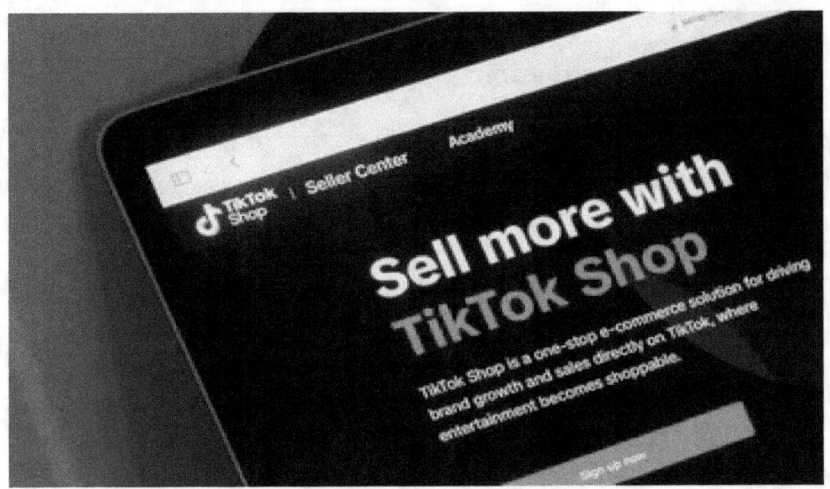

Setting up a TikTok Shop can streamline the purchasing process for users and significantly boost your sales. This chapter will guide you through the steps to create your TikTok Shop, customize your shop's branding and layout, and optimize your product listings.

Creating Your TikTok Shop

Before you can start selling on TikTok, you need to set up and get approved for a TikTok Shop. Here are the steps to do this:

Steps to Apply and Get Approved for a TikTok Shop

1. **Eligibility Check**: Ensure your account meets the eligibility criteria, such as having at least 1,000 followers and being located in an approved TikTok Shop country.

2. **Business Information**: Gather all necessary business information, including your business license, tax information, and bank account details.
3. **Application Submission**: Go to the TikTok for Business website and submit your application for a TikTok Shop. This process includes filling out forms with your business information and agreeing to TikTok's terms and conditions.
4. **Approval Process**: After submission, TikTok will review your application. This process can take a few days to a couple of weeks. Once approved, you'll receive an email notification, and you can start setting up your shop.

Pro Tip: Ensure all information is accurate and complete to avoid delays in the approval process (Social Champ) (Kalodata).

Customizing Your Shop's Branding and Layout

Once approved, the next step is to customize your TikTok Shop to reflect your brand's identity:

1. **Profile Customization**:
    - **Profile Picture**: Use a high-resolution image of your brand logo.
    - **Bio**: Write a compelling bio that clearly states what your shop offers and includes relevant keywords.

2. **Shop Layout**:
    - **Categories**: Organize your products into clear categories to make it easy for users to navigate.
    - **Featured Products**: Highlight your best-selling or new products at the top of your shop to attract attention.

Pro Tip: Use visually appealing and consistent branding elements across your shop to create a professional and cohesive look.

Optimizing Product Listings

Effective product listings are crucial for attracting and converting potential customers. Here's how to optimize your listings:

Writing Compelling Product Descriptions

- **Clear and Concise**: Write clear, concise descriptions that highlight the key features and benefits of your products.
- **Use Keywords**: Incorporate relevant keywords to improve the discoverability of your products in search results.
- **Customer-Centric**: Focus on how the product can solve a problem or enhance the user's life. For example, instead of just listing the features of a skincare product, explain how it can improve their skin health.

Pro Tip: Use bullet points to make your descriptions easy to read and scan.

Best Practices for Product Photography and Pricing Strategies

1. **Product Photography**:
    - **High-Quality Images**: Use high-resolution photos that clearly show the product from multiple angles.
    - **Consistent Style**: Maintain a consistent style and background for all product photos to create a professional look.
    - **Lifestyle Shots**: Include lifestyle shots that show the product in use, helping customers visualize how it fits into their lives.
2. **Pricing Strategies**:
    - **Competitive Pricing**: Research competitor prices and set your prices competitively while ensuring a healthy profit margin.
    - **Promotions and Discounts**: Offer promotions, discounts, and bundle deals to attract customers and encourage purchases.

Pro Tip: Regularly update your product listings with new photos and descriptions to keep them fresh and engaging (Social Champ) (Kalodata).

By following these steps, you can set up a successful TikTok Shop that attracts and converts customers. In the next chapters, we will explore advanced strategies for leveraging TikTok's analytics and expanding your reach through innovative marketing techniques.

Chapter 7: Analyzing and Optimizing Performance

Analyzing your performance on TikTok is crucial for understanding what works and what doesn't. This chapter will guide you through the key metrics to track and how to use this data to optimize your strategy.

Understanding TikTok Analytics

TikTok's analytics tools offer valuable insights into how your content performs, helping you make informed decisions to improve your strategy.

Key Metrics to Track

1. **Video Views**: This metric shows how many times your videos have been watched. A high view count can indicate popular and engaging content.

2. **Growth Rate**: This measures the increase in your follower count over time. A steady growth rate suggests that your content is consistently attracting new viewers.
3. **Engagement**: This includes likes, comments, shares, and saves. High engagement rates indicate that your content resonates with your audience and encourages interaction.

Pro Tip: Focus on engagement rates rather than just view counts. A video with fewer views but higher engagement can be more valuable than one with many views but little interaction (Social Media Dashboard) (Social Champ).

How to Access and Interpret TikTok Analytics Data

1. **Accessing Analytics**:
    - **Switch to a Pro Account**: To access detailed analytics, ensure you have a TikTok Pro account. You can switch by going to your profile settings and selecting "Manage Account," then "Switch to Pro Account."
    - **Navigate to Analytics**: Once you have a Pro account, go to your profile, tap the three dots in the top right corner, select "Creator Tools," and then tap "Analytics."
2. **Interpreting Analytics**:
    - **Overview Tab**: Provides a snapshot of your account's overall performance, including total video views, profile views, and follower growth.

- **Content Tab**: Offers insights into the performance of individual videos, showing metrics like views, average watch time, and traffic sources.
- **Followers Tab**: Provides demographic information about your followers, including gender, location, and activity times.

Pro Tip: Regularly check your analytics to stay updated on performance trends and adjust your strategy accordingly (Social Media Dashboard) (Social Champ) (Kalodata).

Iterating Based on Data

Using your analytics data effectively can help you identify successful content and areas for improvement, enabling you to refine your content strategy.

Using Analytics to Identify Successful Content and Areas for Improvement

1. **Identify Top-Performing Content**:
    - Look for patterns in your most successful videos. What themes, formats, or topics do they share?
    - Note the average watch time and engagement rates. High retention and interaction rates are indicators of successful content.

2. **Spot Weaknesses**:
    - Identify videos with low engagement or short watch times. Analyze what might have gone wrong – was the hook weak, the content too long, or the message unclear?

Adjusting Strategies Based on Performance Insights

1. **Double Down on Success**:
    - Create more content similar to your top performers. If tutorials are popular, make more tutorials. If humor works, add more comedic elements.
2. **Experiment and Iterate**:
    - Don't be afraid to try new things based on your insights. Test different formats, posting times, and themes to see what else might work.
3. **Optimize Posting Schedule**:
    - Use follower activity data to post when your audience is most active. This can significantly increase your chances of engagement and visibility.

Pro Tip: Continuously iterate and experiment with your content. TikTok trends evolve quickly, so staying adaptable is key (Social Media Dashboard) (Social Champ) (Kalodata).

Chapter 8: Engaging with Your Audience

Building and maintaining a strong relationship with your audience is essential for long-term success on TikTok. This chapter explores strategies for engaging with your followers and maximizing real-time interactions through live streams.

Building a Community

Creating a sense of community around your brand can drive engagement and loyalty. Here's how to foster meaningful interactions:

Responding to Comments and Messages

1. **Engage Actively**:
    - **Reply to Comments**: Respond to comments on your videos to show followers that you value their input. This encourages more people to engage with your content.

- **Answer Direct Messages**: Address questions and feedback in your direct messages. Personal responses can build stronger relationships and loyalty.

2. **Use Positive Interactions**:
    - **Highlight Positive Feedback**: Pin positive comments or share user-generated content to celebrate your community and encourage further participation.
    - **Address Criticism Constructively**: Handle negative comments with grace and use constructive criticism to improve your content.

Pro Tip: Consistent engagement shows that you're approachable and attentive, which can significantly boost follower loyalty and interaction (Social Media Dashboard) (Social Champ).

Creating Content that Encourages Interaction and User Participation

1. **Interactive Content**:
    - **Challenges and Duets**: Create challenges and encourage followers to duet with your videos. This not only increases engagement but also spreads your content to a wider audience.
    - **Polls and Questions**: Use TikTok's features to ask questions or create polls. This invites viewers to interact directly with your content.

2. **User-Generated Content (UGC)**:
   - **Feature Followers**: Highlight content created by your followers. This can include duets, reaction videos, or creative uses of your products.
   - **Create a Hashtag**: Encourage your audience to use a specific hashtag for their content related to your brand. This makes it easy to find and share user-generated content.

Pro Tip: Regularly feature and celebrate your followers' contributions. This fosters a sense of community and encourages ongoing participation (Social Media Dashboard) (Social Champ).

Running Live Streams and Q&A Sessions

Live streaming is a powerful tool for real-time engagement and showcasing your products or services. Here's how to make the most of live sessions:

Benefits of Live Streaming for Real-Time Engagement

1. **Direct Interaction**:
   - **Real-Time Feedback**: Live streaming allows for immediate interaction and feedback from your audience, making it a great way to answer questions and address concerns.
   - **Human Connection**: Live sessions can humanize your brand, making you more relatable and trustworthy.

2. **Increased Visibility**:
    - **Algorithm Boost**: TikTok's algorithm often promotes live streams, giving you an opportunity to reach a broader audience.

Tips for Successful Live Sessions and Showcasing Products Live

1. **Plan Ahead**:
    - **Schedule Announcements**: Let your followers know in advance when you'll be going live. Use TikTok posts, stories, and other social media platforms to spread the word.
    - **Prepare Content**: Plan what you'll discuss or showcase during the live session. Having a loose script or outline can help keep the session focused and engaging.
2. **Engage During the Live Stream**:
    - **Interact with Viewers**: Greet viewers by name, answer their questions, and respond to comments. This makes them feel valued and keeps them engaged.
    - **Showcase Products**: Demonstrate your products in action, share behind-the-scenes looks, or offer exclusive discounts to live viewers.
3. **Follow Up**:
    - **Post Highlights**: Share highlights or key moments from your live session on your TikTok profile to reach those who couldn't join live.

- o **Engage Post-Live**: Respond to comments and questions that were posted during the live stream but not addressed at the time.

Pro Tip: Consistency is key. Regular live sessions can build anticipation and keep your audience engaged over the long term (Social Media Dashboard) (Social Champ) (Kalodata).

Chapter 9: Case Studies and Success Stories

Learning from others' successes can provide invaluable insights and inspiration for your own TikTok marketing journey. This chapter features detailed case studies of brands that have effectively used TikTok to achieve significant growth.

Examples of Brands Succeeding on TikTok

Detailed Case Studies of Small and Large Brands That Have Seen Significant Growth Through TikTok

1. **GymShark**

   Overview:
   - **Industry**: Fitness Apparel
   - **Followers**: Over 2 million

Strategy:

- **Trend Participation**: GymShark leveraged TikTok's trend-driven culture by participating in fitness challenges and creating high-energy workout videos.
- **User-Generated Content**: Encouraged followers to share their workout routines wearing GymShark apparel using specific hashtags.
- **Consistent Posting**: Posted frequently to stay relevant and top-of-mind for followers.

Results:

- **Follower Growth**: Grew its TikTok following to over 2 million users.
- **Increased Sales**: Significant boost in online sales due to enhanced brand visibility and engagement.

Key Takeaways:

- **Engagement**: Actively participating in trends and encouraging user-generated content can significantly boost engagement.
- **Consistency**: Regular posting is essential to maintain visibility and relevance on TikTok (Social Media Dashboard) (Kalodata).

2. **Chipotle**

   Overview:

   - **Industry**: Fast Food
   - **Followers**: Over 1.5 million

   Strategy:

   - **Humor and Relatability**: Used humor and relatable content to engage their audience.
   - **Hashtag Challenges**: Created viral campaigns like the #GuacDance challenge, encouraging users to show off their dance moves.
   - **Collaborations**: Partnered with popular TikTok influencers to reach a broader audience.

   Results:

   - **Engagement**: Generated over 250,000 video submissions for the #GuacDance challenge.
   - **Brand Visibility**: Millions of views on their TikTok content, increasing brand engagement and customer interaction.

   Key Takeaways:

   - **Humor**: Relatable and humorous content can significantly enhance engagement.

- Influencer Collaborations: Partnering with influencers can amplify your reach and credibility (Social Champ) (Kalodata).

3. Elf Cosmetics

Overview:

- Industry: Beauty and Cosmetics
- Followers: Over 1.5 million

Strategy:

- Original Music: Created the original song "Eyes. Lips. Face." which went viral.
- User Participation: Encouraged users to create their own videos using the song and hashtag #EyesLipsFace.
- Engaging Content: Shared tutorials, challenges, and user-generated content to keep followers engaged.

Results:

- Viral Campaign: The hashtag #EyesLipsFace garnered millions of views and user-generated videos.
- Increased Sales: Significant uptick in product sales and brand awareness.

Key Takeaways:

- **Creativity**: Original content, such as music, can drive virality.
- **User Involvement**: Encouraging user participation creates a sense of community and boosts engagement (Social Media Dashboard) (Social Champ).

Conclusion

As TikTok continues to grow and evolve, staying ahead of trends and adapting your strategies is crucial for long-term success. Here are some predictions and encouragements for your TikTok journey.

Future Trends and Opportunities on TikTok

Predictions for TikTok's Growth and Evolving Features

1. **Enhanced Shopping Features**: TikTok is likely to introduce more advanced e-commerce features, making it easier for brands to sell directly on the platform. This includes in-app shopping, improved product tagging, and seamless checkout experiences.
2. **Augmented Reality (AR)**: The use of AR filters and effects will become more prevalent, offering brands innovative ways to engage with users and enhance their content.
3. **Personalized Content**: TikTok's algorithm will continue to evolve, offering even more personalized content to users, which can help brands reach their target audience more effectively.

Encouragement to Stay Adaptable and Innovative in Content Strategies

1. **Stay Adaptable**: The social media landscape, especially on platforms like TikTok, is ever-changing. Staying flexible and ready to adapt your strategies based on the latest trends and algorithm changes is key to sustained success.
2. **Innovate Constantly**: Don't be afraid to experiment with new content formats, trends, and features. Innovation keeps your content fresh and engaging, helping you stand out in a crowded marketplace.
3. **Community Engagement**: Building a strong, engaged community around your brand should always be a priority. Interact with your audience, respond to their feedback, and create content that resonates with them.

Appendices

Glossary of TikTok Terms

- **For You Page (FYP)**: The main feed where TikTok users see recommended videos based on their interests.
- **Duet**: A feature that allows users to create a video alongside an existing TikTok video.
- **Hashtag Challenge**: A campaign where users create content around a specific hashtag, often initiated by a brand or influencer.

Resources for Further Learning

- **TikTok Business Learning Center**: Official TikTok resources for businesses, including tutorials and best practices.
- **Marketing Tools**: Tools such as Hootsuite, Later, and Sprout Social for managing and analyzing your TikTok presence.
- **Relevant Courses**: Online courses from platforms like Udemy and Coursera that offer in-depth training on social media marketing and TikTok strategies.

By following the strategies and insights outlined in this book, you'll be well-equipped to navigate the dynamic world of TikTok marketing. Embrace the platform's unique opportunities, stay adaptable, and keep innovating to achieve your business goals on TikTok.

www.ingramcontent.com/pod-product-compliance
Lightning Source LLC
Chambersburg PA
CBHW071844210526
45479CB00001B/279